MW01055589

HUNTING

JOAN LEWIS

Heinemann Library
Chicago, Illinois

© 2006 Heinemann Library
a division of Reed Elsevier Inc.
Chicago, Illinois

Customer Service   888–454–2279

Visit our website at www.heinemannlibrary.com

Photo research by Jill Birschbach
Designed by Joanna Turner
Illustrations by Barry Atkinson
Originated by Ambassador Litho Ltd.
Printed in China by WKT Company Ltd.

10 09 08
10 9 8 7 6 5 4 3 2

Library of Congress Cataloging-in-Publication Data

Lewis, Joan, 1939-
  Hunting / by Joan Lewis.
     v. cm. — (Get going! hobbies)
  Includes index.
  Contents: What is hunting? — The hunt begins — Wild game and fair chase — Hunting
laws and regulations — Clothing and equipment — Firearms — Prepare to hunt — Ready
and aim — Hunting with partners — Shooting wild game — Building a hunting blind —
Competitions — Conservation.
  ISBN 1-4034-6118-X (hardcover) — ISBN 1-4034-6125-2 (pbk.)
  1. Hunting—Juvenile literature. [1. Hunting.] I. Title. II. Series.
  SK35.5.L48 2004
  799.2'028'3—dc22
                              2003025502

Acknowledgments
The author and publisher are grateful to the following for permission to reproduce
copyright material: p. 4 Dale C. Spartas/Corbis; p. 5t Peter Johnson/Corbis; pp. 5b, 7b, 12,
13l, 15, 16, 17, 18, 20, 21, 23, 26 Dale Spartas Photo; p. 6t David Muench/Corbis; p. 6b
Bridgeman Art Library; p. 7t Royalty-free/Corbis; pp. 8, 9, 13r, 29 Corbis; pp. 10, 27 U.S.
Fish and Wildlife Service; p. 14 John E. Gilmore, III/Gilmorephoto; p. 28 D. Robert &
Lorri Franz/Corbis

Cover photograph of hunters by Dale Spartas Photo

Special thanks to Chuck Heard, an experienced hunter and fisher, for his expert comments
that were used to complete this book.

CONTENTS

Some words are shown in bold, **like this.** You can find out what they mean by looking in the glossary.

Hunting is seeking, tracking, **stalking,** or **calling** a wild animal with the intention, or aim, of killing it. People who do not hunt often ask hunters why they hunt. Most hunters say they hunt for one or more of three reasons: for food, to help balance wildlife populations, and to enjoy the challenge of the chase.

Just as there are different reasons for hunting, there are different ways to hunt. Three examples are still hunting, post hunting, and flushing. Still hunting is walking very slowly and quietly through the area where you expect to find **game.** Post hunters stay in one place and wait for game to appear. To flush game, hunters yell, clap, or make other noises to get hiding animals to come into the open. Once a hunter knows the location of an animal, the hunter can stalk it.

HUNTING ETHICS

Federal and state laws control hunting. Many hunters are also guided by certain beliefs about how hunters should behave. These beliefs are called **hunting ethics.** Hunting ethics give hunters a guide of conduct to help them show respect for wildlife, for other hunters, for landowners, and for nonhunters.

This young hunter holds two pheasants he shot. In the United States, hunting season for pheasants is usually in the fall.

WHERE TO HUNT

In the United States, wildlife belongs to all citizens. Hunting is a right, but opportunities to hunt are controlled. Every state has public lands managed by federal and state government that are open to **licensed** hunters during legal **hunting seasons.** To find public hunting lands near you, contact the U.S. Fish & Wildlife Service or your state department of natural resources (DNR). In some states, the DNR is called the department of environmental **conservation.**

Most hunters hunt on privately owned land. If you plan to hunt on private land, you must contact the landowner ahead of time to ask permission to hunt. Tell the landowner when you want to come and what you plan to hunt. Landowners have the right to refuse to allow hunting on their property. **Ethical** hunters respect that right.

No one owns wildlife, but individuals do own the property where wildlife live. Always obey "No Hunting" signs.

HUNTING CLUBS AND EDUCATIONAL EVENTS

There is a lot to learn before you can hunt. This book can get you started, but you cannot learn to hunt correctly, legally, responsibly, and safely on your own. Mistakes in hunting can result in serious injury and even death. You need instruction and guidance from experienced licensed hunters and **certified** hunter safety instructors. Good places to learn to hunt are at hunting clubs or at youth hunting education events. Some of these clubs and events are listed on pages 26 and 31.

Hunting and shooting club activities give you a chance to improve your skills.

THE HUNT BEGINS

People who lived tens of thousands of years ago left clues about their lives. Some of these clues were pictures painted and carved on the walls and ceilings of some caves. Many cave drawings show animals being hunted. It seems hunters have been part of society for thousands of years.

The first hunters may have trapped animals and killed them with clubs. In time they invented weapons that worked from a safer distance. Cave paintings show spears, bows, and arrows.

People in Utah made this wall carving thousands of years ago to record their daily activities.

WEAPONS

The crossbow was the first major improvement in hunting weapons. Hunters used them for years after firearms were invented. Most hunters now use up-to-date firearms. However, modern versions of early hunting weapons are also still used. Some hunters hunt with guns called **muzzleloaders.**

Muzzleloaders and other early weapons are called primitive weapons. Some hunters feel that using primitive weapons instead of modern ones gives animals a greater chance to escape. This provides the hunter with the greatest challenge and is most fair to the animals. States often have special **hunting seasons** and **licenses** for hunters who use primitive weapons.

The Chinese may have been the first to use the crossbow about 2,300 years ago. This artwork from about 1340 features drawings of people preparing to use crossbows.

PURPOSE

For thousands of years, people depended on hunting to live. Hunting was the only way to get meat for food. People also used the skins of the animals they hunted to make clothing and shelter. As farming developed, people began to rely less on wild **game** and more on farm animals for meat. Even when it was no longer necessary for some individuals to hunt to get food, they kept hunting for sport.

About one third of hunters today hunt with a bow at least part of the time. Most states have a special season for bow hunting.

HUNTING FOR SPORT

Descriptions in art and literature show that hunting for sport has been going on at least since ancient Greek and Roman times. By the 1800s some sport hunters were displaying **mounted** animal heads in their homes as **trophies.** This practice still goes on today. Many people are against hunting for trophy. They feel that hunting for trophy is not an **ethical** reason to kill wildlife.

In today's world, hunting is a choice. Some people hunt. Others do not. But everyone has a connection to hunting. Even families with no family members who hunt today have ancestors who needed to hunt in order to survive.

Some hunters feel that using primitive weapons like this muzzleloader is more challenging than using modern firearms.

Ethical hunters know and respect the wild **game** they hunt by practicing **fair chase.** Fair chase is a set of rules that balance the skill and the equipment of the hunter with the hunted animal's natural ability to escape. Some fair chase rules have become laws. One example is a rule against shooting animals confined in a fenced enclosure. In most states it is against the law to break that rule.

States place game into classes. This helps to determine **hunting seasons** and **license** requirements. Two examples of classes are "small game" and "**migratory birds.**" The classes may vary a little from state to state. Many state fish and wildlife divisions offer free wildlife identification books. General information about hunting wild game is often organized according to animal size and **habitat.**

BIG GAME AND SMALL GAME

Deer, elk, moose, and pronghorns, which are a type of antelope, are examples of big game. Big game hunting often involves walking for miles over rugged land to reach an animal's habitat. The minimum age for getting a license to hunt big game varies from state to state. Age requirements and other hunting laws and regulations change often, so hunters should frequently check their state's hunting regulations.

Squirrels and rabbits are common examples of small game. Hunting for small game usually takes less time and effort than big-game hunting. Small game habitats are usually close to where people live. Most hunters first learn how to hunt by hunting small game.

Hunting for food is an ethical reason to hunt. Many hunters compare the taste of squirrel meat to the taste of chicken.

WATERFOWL AND UPLAND GAME BIRDS

Waterfowl are wild birds that live near water. Ducks and geese are two common examples. Hunting waterfowl requires extra equipment. Many waterfowl hunters use decoys and **calls** to attract the birds. A decoy is an artificial bird used to get wild birds closer to hunters.

Quail, pheasants, grouse, mourning doves, and wild turkeys are examples of upland game birds. Although upland means high ground, upland game birds may be found in lowlands, including the areas around water.

HUNTING SEASONS

In order to manage wildlife populations, states have established hunting seasons for wild game. Each state sets its own seasons for each animal or class of animals. An animal can be legally hunted only during this season. Sometimes states set hunting hours, as well as dates. A typical example is the limiting of wild turkey hunting from a half-hour before sunrise to sunset during the months of the fall hunting season.

At night, wild turkeys perch in trees. A tree may hold from one to a dozen or more wild turkeys. To guarantee fair chase, it is against the law to hunt wild turkeys at night.

In the early days of the United States, there were no restrictions on hunting. By the 1800s, many **game** animals, such as buffalo and beaver, were hunted almost into **extinction.** Herds of deer, elk, and pronghorns were nearly wiped out. To **conserve** wildlife for the future, many conservationists and hunters urged the government to pass hunting laws. Today each state department of natural resources regulates hunting in their state and enforces hunting laws.

The purposes of hunting laws are to:

- establish **hunting seasons.**
- establish requirements for getting a hunting **license.**
- establish license fees, which are used to fund wildlife conservation programs.
- ensure equal opportunity to hunt for all hunters, including hunters with physical disabilities.
- limit the equipment and methods that hunters can use.
- limit the number of animals that can be taken at a given period.
- establish safety guidelines that protect hunters and nonhunters.
- define the rules of **fair chase.**

Hunting animals out of season or animals that are protected from hunting are examples of **poaching.** Poachers may be fined and jailed.

Hunters who are 16 years and older must buy federal migratory bird hunting stamps to hunt migratory birds, such as the one pictured here. Some states also require state bird hunting stamps.

Migratory Bird Hunting and Conservation Stamp

Redheads

$15

Void after June 30, 2005

U.S. Department of the Interior

GAME-CHECKING STATIONS

Some states require hunters to stop at game-checking stations before and after hunting deer and certain other animals. Officials at the stations ask hunters questions, including the number of animals they saw. State department of natural resources officials use the information to help them make good decisions about managing wildlife resources.

HUNTER EDUCATION CLASSES

Nearly every state requires that hunters take a hunter education class **certified** by the department of natural resources. The course covers the history of hunting and firearms, firearm safety, **hunting ethics** and responsibility, the rules of fair chase, wildlife identification, and safe ways to handle game. Students learn about the hunter's role in wildlife conservation and management. The course also includes an introduction to bow and other specialty hunting, as well as training in survival, first aid, and water safety.

To pass the course, students must pass a written test. They must also demonstrate safe firearm handling skills. Students who pass the tests receive a certificate. Hunters must show the certificate to purchase a hunting license. Certificates earned in one state are usually honored by other states.

Most hunting licenses must be **renewed.** Licenses may be valid for one day, five days, a year, or another period. Lifetime hunting licenses are available for residents of some states. The cost of a lifetime license is often based on the age of the hunter.

In general, completing a hunter education course qualifies a hunter to purchase hunting licenses as needed. However, hunters who are caught breaking safety rules may be required by law to repeat the course before they are allowed to buy another hunting license.

Comfort and safety are equally important when choosing hunting clothing and equipment. Examples of hunting clothing and equipment are below.

Camouflage clothing. **Camouflage** clothing helps hunters blend in with their surroundings and hide from **game.** However, camouflage also makes it difficult for other hunters to see them. To keep warm, hunters usually dress in layers. Be sure to buy camouflage clothing large enough to wear over other clothes.

Hunter orange cap and vest. Hunter orange is a color easily seen by other hunters. Most states require hunters to wear some solid hunter-orange-colored clothing during some seasons. Some states specify a certain number of square inches of hunter orange that must be worn. A cap alone would not meet most state requirements, but a cap and vest together would.

Shooting glasses. Shooting glasses can prevent serious eye injuries. Injuries can result from a gun that misfires, or fires incorrectly; from wind-blown particles; and from limbs of trees and bushes that whip back as a hunter walks by.

Shooting gloves. Many shooting gloves have the fingers cut off so you can handle the trigger easily. Shooting gloves protect your hands from cold weather. Many are padded in the palm and thumb areas to help cushion your hands from scrapes and from the force of the gun when it fires.

Rubber-bottomed boots. Boots with rubber bottoms help keep feet dry, and rubber holds less human scent than leather-bottomed footwear. Animals do not like the smell of humans. If they smell a human scent where a hunter has stepped, the animals will likely run in the opposite direction.

OTHER EQUIPMENT

If you are planning on **calling** game, you will need to carry one or more calls to **mimic** the sounds of the animal you are hunting. Many hunters also carry binoculars, a small first aid kit, and a water bottle. These are especially necessary when hunting in large areas. If you are going to be hunting in a large wilderness area, learn how to use a compass and take one along. It is easy to get lost while hunting. If you are hunting small game, you may want to use a game bag to carry the game that you kill. You will also need a knife to remove the **entrails** of any animals and a small shovel to bury the entrails.

Hunters use calls to lure animals into showing themselves. This young hunter is using a birdcall.

Many hunters carry binoculars to search for game and to locate other hunters.

STORING CLOTHING AND EQUIPMENT

Use your hunting clothing only for hunting. Store hunting clothing and equipment in unscented storage bags. Put a few twigs, leaves, and grasses that are from your usual hunting area into the bag. Adding these natural items will help mask the human smell. You can also buy products from hunting stores that help cover up human odor.

The rifle is one of the two basic kinds of hunting firearms. The type of rifle pictured below is a .22 **caliber.** It is often chosen as the first hunting gun for young hunters. Some .22 bullets can travel more than a mile. There are several other kinds of rifles, but their parts are similar. In all firearms, the **chamber** is the part that holds a **cartridge** ready to be fired. Together, the parts of a firearm that are used to put a cartridge in the chamber, fire the bullet, and remove the empty casing are called the **action** of the firearm.

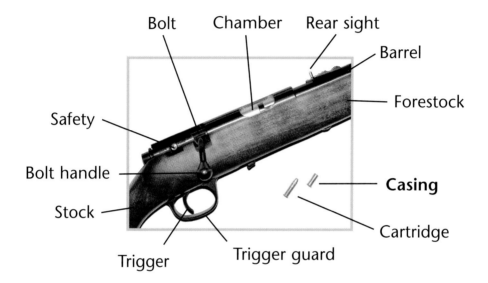

The other basic kind of hunting gun is the shotgun. Shotguns shoot a spray of metal pellets called shot. The further the pellets travel, the more they spread apart. The size of a wound made by a shotgun fired up close is quite large. Shotguns do not usually shoot as far as rifles.

Many hunters prefer a rifle for small **game.** But a .22 rifle does not have the power to kill large game, such as deer. However, many rifles have much more power than a .22. It is important to match both the firearm and the **ammunition** to the game being hunted and to the conditions of the hunt. You can find information to help you do that in books about firearms and hunting.

! FIREARM SAFETY

About 200 young people age nineteen and younger are killed in firearm accidents each year. Follow these safety rules anytime you are around firearms.

- *Never* handle firearms unless you are with an adult.

- *Never* assume that any firearm is unloaded. *Always* check it yourself.

- *Always* treat every firearm as if it is loaded.

- *Never* point a firearm at anything you do not intend to shoot.

- *Always* keep the safety on and your finger off of the trigger when walking with your firearm.

- *Always* keep the action of your shotgun open while walking.

- *Always* use the safety but *never* depend on it. The safety on a firearm can fail.

- *Always* unload your firearm and keep the action open when crossing a fence or whenever you might easily slip or fall.

- *Always* keep firearms unloaded while in a vehicle or boat.

- *Always* store bullets and firearms in separate locations. *Always* lock both.

- *Never* play, push, shove, or joke around while holding firearms.

The shoulder cradle carry is comfortable and safe, but it should not be used if another hunter is walking beside you.

Before you make plans to go on a hunt, follow these steps to prepare to hunt.

1 ***Become physically fit.*** Hunting is hard work. It takes a lot of strength and endurance to walk for miles, especially over rough areas. A hunter who is short of breath will not be able to hold a gun steady enough to take a clean shot. A clean shot strikes a target animal in a vital organ and kills it. An exhausted hunter may be tempted to not follow safety rules and **hunting ethics.** If you are in good health, train to get physically fit. If you are a hunter with physical disabilities, find out about special hunting permits, **licenses,** and opportunities in your state.

2 ***Become mentally ready.*** Hunting is a personal decision. Only you can decide if you are ready to hunt. Never let anyone bully or shame you into hunting if you are not ready.

3 ***Practice shooting.*** You need to be a good shot to avoid wounding your target instead of killing it. The only way to get a feel for the range of your gun is to shoot it in a safe, adult-supervised situation.

Following hunting ethics means you need to develop your shooting skills before going out on hunts.

PLANNING A SPECIFIC HUNT

When planning a hunt, prepare for the hunting day or trip by following these steps.

1 *Check the season.* Make sure that your intended **game** is in season.

2 *Learn about your intended game.* Be certain you know exactly what both the male and female and the young of the animal look like. Know which you are allowed to hunt legally.

3 *Plan the date of the hunt with your adult hunting partner.* Never go hunting without an adult licensed hunter.

4 *Gather appropriate equipment.* The hunting of some game requires more equipment than others. When you are getting your clothing ready, consider the weather along with safety. Wear clothes that will keep you comfortable and safe. To avoid a dangerous health hazard known as hypothermia, it is important to not get chilled while hunting. Hypothermia occurs when your body loses heat faster than it can produce heat.

5 *Get appropriate license, tags, and stamps.* Check with your state department of natural resources to see what is required.

6 *Get permission to hunt.* If you plan to hunt on private property, ask for permission ahead of time.

Hunters of ducks and other birds that migrate must register with the Migratory Bird Harvest Information Program (HIP) before they hunt. This program keeps track of the types and numbers of migratory birds taken by hunters.

READY AND AIM

If you cannot hold the gun steady, it is not safe to shoot. The four basic shooting positions are shown below. Some hunters rest the hand or elbow supporting the gun on a tree, rock, or other solid object. Never rest your gun directly on an object. Doing so lessens your control of the **muzzle**.

- Prone (most steady position)

1. Lie so your body is just to the left of where you want to aim. 2. Place your left elbow just to the left of your rifle. 3. Bending your right leg at the knee and placing your right foot over your left leg may make you steadier.

- Sitting (second steadiest position)

1. Sit on firm ground. 2. Place your legs just to the right of the direction you are aiming. 3. Rest your elbows on your knees.

- Kneeling (third steadiest position)

1. Sit on the back of your right foot. 2. Hold your body about 45 degrees to the left of where you want to aim. 3. Support your left elbow with your left knee.

- Standing (least steady position)

1. Stand sideways with your feet parallel to the direction you are aiming. 2. Spread your legs to about the width of your shoulders.

AIM

To shoot accurately, aim using your dominant eye, or your strongest eye. To find your dominant eye, form a triangle with your hands. Hold your hands with palms facing outward, place one thumb over the other, and touch your index fingers together. Then stretch your arms out away from your face. Look through the triangular opening and focus on an object in the distance. Close one eye at a time. Your weak eye will see the back of one of your hands. Your dominant eye will be focused on the object. For most people, the dominant eye is the same as the dominant hand. If you are right-handed, your right eye is probably dominant.

To aim correctly, look through the rear **sight** of your gun. Put the front sight in the middle of the target. Then line up the back sight with the front sight.

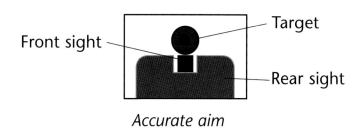

Accurate aim

Inaccurate, bullet will go right of target *Inaccurate, bullet will go left of target* *Inaccurate, bullet will go over target* *Inaccurate, bullet will go in front of target*

To aim an **aperture sight,** center the target in the peephole on the rear sight, then line up the target with the front sight. To aim a **telescopic sight,** line up the target where the crosshairs cross in the sight.

One thing to remember about aiming is that rifle bullets do not travel in a straight line. Gravity causes them to travel in an arc. Another thing to remember is that to hit a moving target, you must aim slightly ahead of the target. You will need a lot of practice to learn to aim accurately.

HUNTING WITH PARTNERS

Hunting laws set minimum age limits for hunting alone. If you are under this age, you must hunt with an adult with a hunting **license.** For safety, it is best to have no more than three hunters in a group. It is important to never lose sight of your hunting partners. Never separate. To prevent accidents, always walk beside one another when you might shoot.

Before you begin to hunt, decide with your partner what you will do if you become separated. It is always helpful to have a map of the hunting area and to become familiar with it before the hunt.

If you lose sight of your hunting partner, unload your gun and stop hunting until you find your partner.

ESTABLISHING A SAFE ZONE OF FIRE

The area into which a hunter can shoot safely is called a safe zone of fire. Each hunter has a personal safe zone of fire about 45 degrees in front of him or her. Every time you move, your safe zone of fire changes. Keep aware of where it is as you walk.

When hunting with partners, hunters should be about the length of a basketball court apart. This distance allows each hunter to have a safe zone of fire.

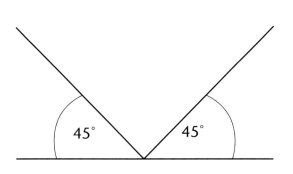

Hold your arms out at the angle shown here to estimate your safe zone of fire. Look straight ahead. Move your arms straight in until you can see both of your thumbs without moving your eyes. Your thumbs mark the edges of your safe zone of fire.

Every time you take a step, your safe zone of fire can change.

SHOOTING WILD GAME

Before you shoot . . .

| √ | ***Check your partners.*** Are you certain where they are? |

| √ | ***Check your target.*** Are you certain that what you are about to shoot is the animal you are hunting? |

| √ | ***Check your range.*** Is the target animal close enough for you to make a clean shot? |

| √ | ***Check for anything in the way.*** Is there anything between you and the target that could cause your bullet to **ricochet?** |

| √ | ***Check the background.*** Can you see where the bullet will stop if you miss? Will something in the background safely stop the bullet? |

| √ | ***Check your footing.*** Do you have a firm place to position yourself and take a steady aim? |

| √ | ***Check your safe zone of fire.*** Are you shooting within your safe zone of fire? |

| √ | ***Check your feelings.*** Do you feel right about taking this animal at this time? |

Once you squeeze the trigger, there is no going back. If the animal is wounded and runs, it is **unethical** to let it suffer. You must follow the animal and kill it to put an end to its suffering.

WHEN NOT TO SHOOT

Never shoot . . .

- If you have lost sight of your hunting partners.
- If you have any doubt of your target.
- If you think the target may be out of range.
- If you can see something that might cause your bullet to ricochet.
- If you cannot see beyond your target.
- If you cannot hold the gun steady enough to aim well.
- If you must shoot outside your safe zone of fire.
- If you do not feel right about taking this animal at this particular time.

AFTER THE KILL

Be cautious when approaching an animal you think is dead. If the animal is only stunned, it could cause you serious harm. Some hunters recommend poking the animal in the eye with a long stick to be sure the animal is not still alive.

Cleaning game in the field is recommended. Removing the **entrails** helps cool the meat, which helps prevent spoiling. To control smell and prevent other animals from eating them, bury the entrails.

Some Native Americans who hunt pause to appreciate the animal they have taken. Many other hunters do this, too.

BUILDING A HUNTING BLIND

Hunters often use blinds when hunting turkey, ducks, deer, or other game. Blinds are shelters that hide hunters from wildlife. Hunting blinds are a good choice only where there is a lot of target **game** and you know it is likely to come to the blind location.

Follow these directions to build a portable two-hunter blind at the hunting site. You can take apart and rebuild this blind over and over. Get an adult to help you gather the supplies and build the blind.

Materials:

(4) 6-foot (1.8-meter) pieces of CPVC 3/4-inch (2-centimeter) pipe (sold in home improvement stores)

(8) 4-foot (1.2-meter) pieces of CPVC 3/4-inch (2-centimeter) pipe

(8) CPVC elbow joints each with (2) 3/4-inch (2-centimeter) openings and (1) 1/2-inch (1.3-centimeter) opening

(10) 6-inch (15-centimeter) bungee cords with hooks at both ends

(1) roll of duct tape

(1) piece of **camouflage** material* about 60 inches (1.53 meters) x 15 feet (4.6 meters) (sold in hunting supply stores)

* Camouflage material comes in various patterns and forms. Some has slits in it to be used for pointing firearms out of the blind. Some material is thin enough to see through. Some has scent blockage to help block human scent.

You might prefer to wrap netting around your blind frame and stick grasses, leaves, or branches in the netting to create a natural camouflage.

Building Directions:

1 Choose a place to build your blind. For protection, place the blind so your back is to a hill, large tree, or rock.

2 Use four elbow joints, two 6-foot (1.8-meter) pipes, and two 4-foot (1.2-meter) pipes to make a square, as shown below. Tape the joints.

3 Repeat Step 2 using the same size and number of parts.

4 Use the remaining four 4-foot (1.2-meter) pieces to join the squares and make a box, as shown below. Tape the joints.

5 Drape the camouflage material around the box, as shown below. The open entrance should face a hill, tree, or rock.

6 Hook one end of the bungee cords into the overlapped material. Pull other end of cord and hook into the side material as shown below. Place cords about 18 inches (46 centimeters) apart.

7 If needed, cut 18-inch (46-centimeter) vertical shooting slits in the front and sides as shown.

½" opening

¾" openings

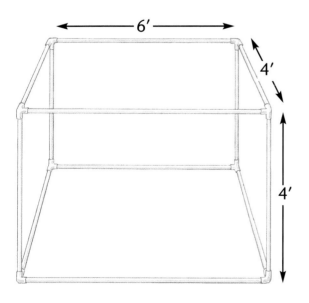

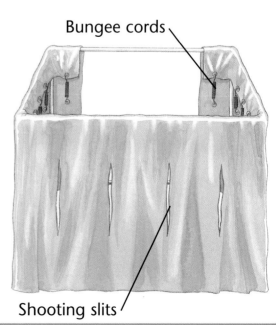

Bungee cords

Shooting slits

Local hunting and shooting clubs hold hunting and shooting events for young people. Many of the events test hunter education knowledge and skills. Shooting skills are also tested. These type of competitive events give young hunters a chance to show what they have learned and see how they measure up against their peers.

YOUTH HUNTER EDUCATION CHALLENGE

The National Rifle Association (NRA) sponsors the Youth Hunter Education Challenge (YHEC) every year. The YHEC is held at the regional, state, national, and international levels. The competition is open to any person under the age of nineteen who has completed a certified hunter education course. YHEC participants test their hunting skills in the following events: .22 rifle, shotgun, **muzzleloader,** archery, **orienteering,** wildlife identification, and hunter responsibility. All the shooting events are designed to **simulate** actual hunting situations as closely as possible. There is also a written hunter safety exam.

4-H SHOOTING SPORTS RANGE COMPETITION

4-H is a national organization dedicated to youth education. Many local 4-H clubs sponsor the 4-H Shooting Sports Program. This program teaches young people the safe and responsible use of firearms. The basic principles of hunting and archery are also taught. Competitions for people who have been part of the program are held each year at the local, regional, state, and national levels.

Showing that you can use firearms safely is an important achievement.

JUNIOR DUCK STAMP COMPETITION

Each year wildlife artists compete to design the federal duck stamp. Hunters sixteen years and older who want to hunt **migratory birds** are required by law to purchase such a stamp in addition to their hunting **licenses.** There is also a competition for young people. Schools in every state can participate in the junior duck stamp design contest. The contest is held every year in each state. To enter, you must use paints, pastels, or other materials to create a picture of one of the waterfowl from the contest list.

In each state, a best of show entry is chosen from the state winners. The best of show from each state competes in a national contest. The national winner's design is used to produce the federal junior duck stamp for the year. The money from the sale of the junior duck stamps is used to support **conservation** education.

Adam Nisbett from St. James, Missouri, won the federal junior duck stamp contest with the above painting in 2004.

CONSERVATION

The goal of **conservation** is to make sure that **renewable resources,** including wildlife, are managed wisely. When a wildlife population gets so small that it is in danger of becoming **extinct,** it is declared **endangered.** It is against the law to hunt endangered animals. One reason animal populations decline is because their **habitat** has been taken over by people. Local hunting clubs join other conservation organizations in protecting wildlife by setting aside vast amounts of habitat. By respecting **hunting seasons** and limits, hunters help with conservation efforts by leaving enough members of an animal population for it to survive.

REDUCING WILDLIFE POPULATIONS

If conditions are right, some wildlife populations thrive. They increase until the habitat can no longer support them. The animals cannot find enough food to stay healthy. Diseased animals may infect other animals. They crowd other wildlife out of the area. They may destroy or eat certain types of plants until all of those plants are gone. When wildlife overpopulation becomes a problem, hunting helps manage the wildlife. Hunters reduce overpopulation.

Many areas hold special hunts to reduce local herds of white tail deer.

INFORMATION

Hunters also help conservation efforts by providing important information from the field. Hunters take part in surveys, such as the Migratory Bird Harvest Information Program (HIP). They stop at game-checking stations to answer questions about the wildlife they have seen. Hunters also provide samples of the animals they have taken. Wildlife managers test the samples to see how healthy the animal was. Wildlife managers rely on hunters for much of the information needed to make wildlife management decisions.

MONEY

The cost of conservation is high, and hunters pay a lot of those costs. The money hunters spend on **licenses,** tags, and stamps and the taxes they pay on hunting equipment and **ammunition** is used for conservation programs. These programs benefit many types of wildlife, including wildlife that is not typically hunted.

Each year, close to $200 million in federal taxes that hunters pay are used to support wildlife management programs. Also, hunter's organizations raise millions of dollars for returning habitats to their natural conditions, wildlife research, and environmental education.

Conserving wildlife is everyone's responsibility.

GLOSSARY

action	parts of a firearm that place the cartridge in the chamber, fire the bullet, and remove the casing
ammunition	objects fired from firearms
aperture sight	sight that uses a small, circular hole to allow hunters to aim and shoot at animals
caliber	inside diameter of a gun barrel. A diameter is a line passing through the center of a circle.
calling	luring wildlife into the open by imitating its cries. A call is an instrument that mimics the sounds of a particular animal.
camouflage	materials or colors and patterns in clothes that help hunters blend with the surroundings
cartridge	ammunition for firearm
casing	part of a cartridge that holds gunpowder
certify	to authorize or permit by license
chamber	part of a firearm that holds a cartridge ready to be fired
conservation	careful protection and preservation of nature
endangered	at risk of becoming extinct
entrails	internal organs of an animal
ethical	following accepted rules of good conduct
extinction	end of existence
fair chase	set of rules that balance the hunter's skill and equipment with the animal's natural ability to escape
game	wildlife hunted for food or sport
habitat	natural surroundings where a wild animal lives
hunting ethics	beliefs about how hunters should behave
hunting season	time during which specific wildlife can be legally hunted
license	tag or document showing that an individual has legal permission to do something
migratory bird	bird that travels from one region to another according to season
mimic	to imitate
mounted	stuffed and prepared in order to display on a wall
muzzleloader	primitive firearm that is loaded through the muzzle. The muzzle is the end of a gun from which a bullet is shot.
orienteering	contest in which contestants use a map and compass to find their way through unfamiliar territory
poaching	illegal hunting; hunting outside of hunting laws
renewable resources	valuable things found in nature that are replaced in natural cycles or by conservationists
ricochet	to bounce at least once at an angle from a surface
sight	device on firearms that helps the eye in aiming
simulate	to give the appearance of or make similar to
stalking	sneaking up on an animal to get close to it
telescopic sight	sight that uses a telescope to allow hunters to aim and shoot at animals
trophy	token from a successful hunt that is taken and saved

MORE BOOKS TO READ

Armentrout, David. *Hunting.* Vero Beach, Fla.: Rourke Publishing, 1998.

Frahm, Randy. *Duck Hunting.* Mankato, Minn.: Capstone Press, 2002.

Painter, Doug. *The Field and Stream Firearms Safety Handbook.* Guilford, Conn.: Globe Pequot Press, 1999.

Weaver, Jack. *Hunting: Have Fun, Be Smart.* New York: Rosen Publishing, 2003.

Weintraub, Aileen. *Bow Hunting.* Mankato, Minn.: Capstone Press, 2004.

TAKING IT FURTHER

International Hunter Education Association
P.O. Box 490
3725 Cleveland Ave.
Wellington, CO 80549
info@ihea.com

National Hunting
and Fishing Day Headquarters
11 Mile Hill Road
Newtown, CT 06470-2359
nhfday@nssf.org

National Muzzle Loading Rifle Association
P.O. Box 67
Friendship, IN 47021
(812) 667-5131

National Rifle Association of America
Youth Hunter Education Challenge
Hunter Services Department
11250 Waples Mill Road
Fairfax, VA 22030
(703) 267-1500

United States Fish and Wildlife Service
1849 C Street NW
Washington, D.C. 20240
(800) 344-9453

INDEX